Where does the Money go

Lucie Dupont

Lucie Dupont

Lucie Dupont

Lucie Dupont

Index

Lucie Dupont

Introduction to Money Loss

Have you ever wondered where your money goes each month? It seems like as soon as it hits your account, it disappears like magic. This is a common experience for many people. What happens is that, without realizing it, we make small expenses that, accumulated, represent a significant part of our income. This phenomenon is known as "invisible money loss." Throughout this chapter, we will explore how these expenses go unnoticed and how we can take control to avoid losing money without realizing it.

Imagine that you have a bucket full of water, but with small leaks. At first, it doesn't seem like much, just a few drops here and there. However, over time, the water level begins to drop considerably. The same goes for our money. A coffee here, an impulse purchase there, and before we know it, our financial bucket is half empty.

One of the biggest culprits of invisible money loss is small daily expenses. You might think buying a $3 coffee every day isn't a big deal, but when you add it up, it's $90 a month and more than $1,000 a year. These expenses, which seem insignificant at the time, add up quickly. It's easy to justify a small purchase because it doesn't seem like it will make a big difference, but the reality is that these expenses can add up and have a significant impact on our budget.

Invisible subscriptions are another big hole in our financial bucket. Streaming services, apps, gym memberships, and other subscriptions we don't use regularly may be draining our money. Many times, we forget about these subscriptions and continue paying for them month after month. A regular review of all subscriptions can reveal unnecessary expenses that we can eliminate to save money.

Banking fees and commissions also contribute to invisible money loss. ATM withdrawal fees, account maintenance, and overdraft fees are some examples. These costs may seem small, but they add up quickly. Opting for bank accounts that do not charge fees and being attentive to the conditions of our credit cards can help us avoid these expenses.

Impulse purchases are another example of how we lose money without realizing it. You walk into a store to buy one thing and leave with five items you didn't plan to buy. These purchases may seem harmless, but if they become a habit, they can seriously affect your budget. Adopting the 24-hour rule, where you wait a day before making an impulse purchase, can help you reduce these expenses.

The cost of convenience also plays a big role in losing money. Paying extra for services like food delivery, laundry, and transportation can be convenient, but also expensive. While these services may save time, it is important to evaluate whether it is really worth the additional cost. Planning and preparing meals at home, and finding cheaper transportation alternatives can help you reduce these expenses.

Not planning purchases is another common mistake. Buying without a list or without planning can lead to unnecessary expenses and waste. Creating shopping lists and planning big purchases in advance can help you avoid impulse purchases and save money.

Inefficient use of resources can also drain your money. Waste of electricity, water and gas can result in high bills. Implementing energy efficiency practices and responsible use of resources can help you reduce these costs.

Not comparing prices is a mistake that can cost you a lot of money. Not looking for the best deal or comparing prices before purchasing can lead you to overpay for products and services. Using price comparators and looking for deals and discounts can help you get the best value for your money.

In short, invisible money loss is a common problem that affects many people. Identifying and addressing these small expenses can make a big difference in your budget. Throughout this book, we will explore various strategies to avoid losing money and take control of your finances. Remember, every little savings counts, and over time, those small changes can result in big financial improvements. Let's find out where our money goes and how we can keep it in our pocket!

Small Daily Expenses

Imagine a typical day: you wake up, get ready to go to work, and on the way, you stop to buy a coffee. Then, mid-morning, you realize you need a snack and buy a snack from the vending machine. At lunch time, you decide to eat out because you didn't bring food from home. Later, after work, you stop by the store to buy some things you think you need, but end up taking a few extras. Finally, you decide to order food delivery because you are too tired to cook. These small daily expenses may seem insignificant individually, but they add up quickly and can make up a sizable chunk of your monthly budget.

Small daily expenses are like small cracks in a dam. At first, it doesn't seem like a big deal. A coffee here, a snack there, and a quick meal now and then don't seem to do much harm. But when you add up all these expenses at the end of the month, you realize that you have spent much more than you thought. A $3 coffee a day may seem harmless, but at the end of the month, it's $90 and at the end of the year, more than $1,000. The same goes for snacks and meals away from home. Every small purchase contributes to a large sum of money that you could have saved or used more efficiently.

One of the reasons these small expenses are so damaging is because we are not fully aware of them. It's easy to lose count of how many coffees, snacks and fast foods we buy in a week. Additionally, since these expenses are small, we don't feel like they are affecting our finances in any significant way. But the truth is, by not keeping track of these expenses, we miss the opportunity to identify areas where we could save money.

So how can we take control of these small daily expenses? The first solution is to keep a record of all our expenses, no matter how small they may be. You can use a notebook, an app on your phone, or even a spreadsheet. The important thing is to write down each expense, no matter how insignificant it may seem. This practice will help you become aware of how much you are really spending and will allow you to identify patterns and areas where you could reduce expenses.

Another effective strategy is to create a budget and stick to it. Allocate a specific amount of money for daily expenses and make sure you don't exceed that limit. Not only will this help you control your spending, but it will also make you think twice before making an impulse purchase. If you know that you only have a limited amount of money to spend on coffees and snacks, you will be more selective with your purchases.

Planning ahead is also key to reducing small daily expenses. Making your coffee at home and taking it with you in a thermos can save you a lot of money throughout the month. The same goes for snacks and meals. Preparing your own meals and bringing them to work is not only cheaper, but it's also healthier. Plus, you can save time by not having to go out to buy food.

Avoiding impulse purchases is another way to reduce small daily expenses. It's easy to be tempted to buy things we don't need when we're in a store. To avoid this, make a shopping list before you leave the house and stick to it. This will help you buy only what you need and avoid unnecessary expenses.

Another useful tactic is the 24-hour rule. If you see something you want to buy but aren't sure if you really need it, wait 24 hours before purchasing it. This waiting time will give you the opportunity to reflect on whether you really need that item or if it is just a momentary whim. Many times, after 24 hours, you will realize that you can do without that purchase.

In short, small daily expenses may seem insignificant, but they add up quickly and can significantly affect your budget. By keeping track of your expenses, creating a budget, planning ahead, and avoiding impulse purchases, you can take control of these small expenses and save a considerable amount of money. Remember, every little savings counts, and at the end of the month, those small changes can make a big difference in your finances. It's time to take control of your daily expenses and keep more money in your pocket!

Lucie Dupont

Invisible Subscriptions

Have you ever wondered why your money disappears so quickly from your bank account? One of the most common culprits is invisible subscriptions. These are those subscriptions that we forget we have or simply don't use, but they continue to charge us each month. Throughout this chapter, we'll explore how these subscriptions can drain your finances without you realizing it and how you can take control to eliminate them and save money.

Invisible subscriptions are like little holes in your pocket. At first, they may not seem like a big deal. You pay a small amount each month for a streaming service, a fitness app, or a gym membership. However, when you add up all these subscriptions, you realize that you are spending a lot more than you thought. These small monthly charges add up and can represent a significant portion of your monthly expenses.

One of the problems with invisible subscriptions is that they are easy to forget. When you sign up for a service, it's often to take advantage of a special offer or a free trial period. Once the trial period ends, automatic charging begins, and if you're not paying attention, you may not even realize you're being charged. Subscriptions to streaming services, apps, digital magazines, and other online services are common examples of these types of expenses.

To take control of your invisible subscriptions, the first step is to identify them. Review your bank and credit card statements carefully to see all recurring charges. Make a list of all the subscriptions you find. This exercise can be revealing, as you might discover that you are paying for services that you don't even remember signing up for. Once you have the list, evaluate each subscription and ask yourself if you really need and use it.

Canceling unnecessary subscriptions is the next step. It can be tedious, but it is a necessary task to prevent your money from continuing to go on services that you do not use. Some services can make canceling a little complicated, but persevere and follow the necessary steps to unsubscribe. It's also helpful to set reminders on your calendar to review and cancel subscriptions before they automatically renew.

In addition to canceling unnecessary subscriptions, consider consolidating services. For example, if you have multiple subscriptions to streaming services, evaluate which one you use the most and cancel the others. Many times, a single service can offer most of the content you want. There are also bundling options that can be cheaper than maintaining multiple separate subscriptions.

Another approach to managing invisible subscriptions is to use tools and applications designed to manage your subscriptions. There are several apps that can help you identify and cancel unwanted subscriptions. These tools allow you to see all your subscriptions in one place and notify you when a subscription is about to renew, giving you the opportunity to cancel it if you no longer need it.

Automation can be both a blessing and a curse. While it's convenient to not have to worry about manually paying for each subscription, it also makes it easy to forget those subscriptions are there. To avoid this, do a regular review of all your subscriptions, perhaps every three to six months. This review will help you stay aware of what you are spending your money on and allow you to make adjustments as necessary.

In short, invisible subscriptions are one of the most common ways we lose money without realizing it. By identifying, evaluating, and canceling unnecessary subscriptions, you can save a considerable amount of money each month. Consolidating services and using subscription management tools can also help you stay on top of your spending. Remember, every little savings counts, and at the end of the month, those small changes can make a big difference in your finances. It's time to take control of your invisible subscriptions and keep more money in your pocket!

Lucie Dupont

Bank Fees and Commissions

Have you ever looked at your statement and been surprised to see multiple small charges that you weren't expecting? These charges are typically bank fees and commissions, which can add up quickly and significantly impact your finances. Although they may seem insignificant individually, added together they can represent a considerable amount of money that you could be putting to better use. In this chapter, we will explore how to identify these fees, understand their impact, and take steps to reduce or eliminate them.

Bank fees and commissions can come in many forms and are often hidden in the fine print of banking contracts. Among the most common are account maintenance fees, ATM withdrawal charges, overdraft fees, and wire transfer fees. Although these charges may seem small, if they add up month after month, they can add up to a large amount of money at the end of the year. For example, an account maintenance fee of $10 per month is $120 per year.

One of the first steps to reducing these fees is to understand exactly why and when you are being charged. Review your bank statements regularly and write down any charges you don't understand. If you see recurring fees, such as account maintenance or overdraft fees, investigate why they are being applied. Most banks have detailed guides explaining their fees and commissions, and you can find them on their websites or request them at a branch.

An effective way to avoid bank fees is to opt for accounts that don't charge them. Many banks offer checking and savings accounts with no maintenance fees, especially if you meet certain requirements, such as maintaining a minimum balance or setting up regular direct deposits. Research and compare the options available at different banks to find the one that best suits your needs. Switching banks may seem inconvenient, but the long-term savings can be significant.

ATM withdrawal fees are another common source of unnecessary expenses. Any time you use an ATM outside of your bank's network, you'll likely be charged a fee. To avoid these fees, plan ahead and only use your own bank's ATMs. Another option is to look for banks that reimburse ATM fees, a benefit some offer as part of their accounts.

Overdraft fees are another charge that can add up quickly. An overdraft occurs when you spend more money than you have in your account, and the bank covers the difference, but charges you a fee for this service. To avoid these charges, keep close tabs on your bank balance and set up alerts to notify you when your balance is low. You can also link your checking account to a savings account as a backup to cover any overdrafts, often without additional fees.

Bank transfers, both domestic and international, can be expensive due to fees charged by banks. If you make frequent transfers, investigate the options available to reduce these costs. Some banks offer free or low-cost transfers if done online rather than in a branch. Additionally, there are online money transfer services that are often cheaper than traditional banks.

Another way to reduce bank fees is to take advantage of the promotions and benefits that banks offer. Some banks offer fee waivers for students, retirees, or holders of certain premium accounts. Find out if you qualify for any of these options and take advantage of the benefits available.

Additionally, maintaining open communication with your bank can be helpful. If you see unexpected charges on your account, don't hesitate to contact your bank and ask about them. In some cases, the bank may be willing to waive one-time charges, especially if you are a long-standing customer. You can also negotiate with your bank to reduce or eliminate certain fees, especially if you have a good banking history.

In short, bank fees and commissions may seem insignificant, but they add up quickly and affect your finances. By understanding why these fees apply, opting for accounts that don't charge them, planning for ATM use, avoiding overdrafts, and taking advantage of promotions, you can significantly reduce these expenses. Remember, every little savings counts, and at the end of the month, those small changes can make a big difference in your finances. It's time to take control of your banking fees and keep more money in your pocket!

27

Lucie Dupont

Impulse Purchases

Have you ever walked into a store with the intention of buying just one item and walked out with a bag full of things you didn't plan to buy? We've all been there. Impulse purchases are those expenses that we make in the moment, without really thinking about whether we need or can afford those items. Although they may seem harmless at the time, impulsive purchases can quickly add up and seriously affect our finances. In this chapter, we'll explore why we make impulse purchases, how they affect our budget, and how we can control them to save money.

Impulsive purchases are often the result of emotional rather than rational decisions. It's easy to get carried away by an attractive offer, a "buy one, get one free" promotion, or simply the desire to treat ourselves. Stores are designed to encourage this behavior. From the strategic placement of products on shelves to the lights and music, everything is designed to make us buy more. Even online shopping is full of tactics designed to get us to add more things to our shopping cart, like suggestions for related products and limited-time offers.

One of the main problems with impulse buying is that we often buy things we don't really need. These items may end up forgotten in a closet or, worse yet, be used only once before being thrown away. This is not only a waste of money, but also a waste of resources. Additionally, impulsive purchases can lead us to spend more than we planned, which can cause financial stress and difficulty meeting other financial commitments.

To control impulse purchases, the first step is to recognize when and why we make these purchases. Keeping track of your daily expenses can help you identify patterns. Do you tend to make impulse purchases when you're stressed, bored, or simply because something is on sale? Once you understand your triggers, you can take steps to avoid them.

An effective strategy to reduce impulse purchases is the 24-hour rule. If you see something you want to buy, but you're not sure if you really need it, wait 24 hours before making the purchase. This waiting time will give you the opportunity to reflect on whether you really need that item or if it is just a momentary whim. Many times, after 24 hours, you will realize that you can do without that purchase.

Another useful technique is to make a shopping list and stick to it. Before you go to the store, make a list of the items you really need and commit to not buying anything that isn't on the list. Not only will this help you avoid impulse purchases, but it will also save you time by not wandering the aisles of the store. When shopping online, use the same technique. Make a list of what you need and avoid browsing the offers and promotions pages.

Budget also plays a crucial role in controlling impulse purchases. Allocate a specific amount of money for discretionary spending each month and commit to not exceeding that limit. Not only will this help you control your spending, but it will also make you think twice before making an impulse purchase. If you know you only have a limited amount of money to spend on treats, you'll be more selective with your purchases.

Planning large purchases in advance is another way to avoid impulse purchases. If you know you need to buy something expensive, like an appliance or piece of furniture, do your research in advance, compare prices and wait for sales or promotions to make the purchase. Not only will this allow you to get the best price, but it will also give you time to reflect on whether you really need that item.

The "spend now, pay later" mentality is another factor that contributes to impulse purchases. Credit cards and deferred payment options make it easy to buy things without thinking about the immediate financial consequences. To avoid this, try using cash or debit cards for your daily purchases. This will help you be more aware of how much you are spending and avoid the temptation to spend more than you can afford.

Finally, it is important to remember that it is okay to treat yourself from time to time, as long as it is within your financial means. It's not about depriving yourself of all the things you love, but about being conscious of your purchasing decisions and making sure you are spending your money in a way that benefits you in the long term.

In short, impulse purchases are a common habit that can seriously affect your budget. By recognizing your triggers, using strategies like the 24-hour rule, making shopping lists, setting a budget, and planning ahead, you can take control of your impulsive spending. Remember, every little savings counts, and at the end of the month, those small changes can make a big difference in your finances. It's time to take control of your impulse purchases and keep more money in your pocket!

Lucie Dupont

The Cost of Convenience

We live in an era where convenience is king. Everything is designed to make our lives easier: from food delivery apps to stores that offer quick shopping services. However, this convenience comes at a cost that often goes unnoticed. In this chapter, we'll explore how convenience expenses can quickly add up, affecting your finances, and what steps you can take to minimize these costs without sacrificing too much of your comfort.

Convenience comes in many forms. Think about the number of times you have ordered food delivery instead of cooking at home, or how many times you have used a washing and ironing service instead of doing it yourself. These services are incredibly useful, especially when time is tight, but they are also more expensive than DIY alternatives. A home-delivered meal, for example, can cost double or more than if you prepare it at home. Delivery charges, tips, and inflated convenience costs add up quickly.

One of the most common places where we pay for convenience is at the supermarket. Pre-cut, pre-cooked and packaged foods are significantly more expensive than their fresh, unprocessed versions. A pre-packaged salad can cost three times as much as the ingredients needed to make the same salad at home. Supermarkets know that we will pay more to not have to wash, cut and prepare our food, and they take advantage of this provision.

Transportation is another area where we pay for convenience. Using transportation apps like Uber or Lyft can be much more expensive than using public transportation. Although it may be tempting to take a quick, comfortable ride instead of waiting for the bus, these additional costs add up quickly. Even driving your own car has its own hidden convenience costs, like parking and gas.

Subscriptions and streaming services are another clear example. Services like Netflix, Spotify, and Amazon Prime offer incredible convenience by providing entertainment and shopping at your fingertips. However, maintaining multiple subscriptions can add up to a significant amount of money each month. Many times, we pay for services that we do not use regularly, simply because it is convenient to have access to them when we want them.

To control the cost of convenience, the first step is to be aware of these expenses. Keeping track of all convenience-related expenses can be eye-opening. Write down every food delivery order, every Uber ride, and every pre-cut grocery item you buy. At the end of the month, add up these expenses and ask yourself if they were really worth it in terms of time and comfort.

An effective strategy to reduce these costs is to plan ahead. If you know you're going to have a busy week, prepare meals ahead of time and freeze them. This way, you can avoid the temptation of ordering food at home. Instead of relying on transportation services for convenience, plan your time to use public transportation or, if possible, carpool with friends or coworkers.

The kitchen is an area where you can save a lot of money with a little planning. Buy fresh foods and prepare your own meals. Not only will you save money, but you will also eat healthier. Spending a couple of hours on the weekend preparing meals for the week can significantly reduce the need to buy pre-cooked foods or order takeout.

Reevaluating your subscriptions can also be very beneficial. Make a list of all the services you subscribe to and ask yourself if you really use them all. Cancel those you don't use regularly and consider sharing subscriptions with family or friends to reduce costs. Many streaming platforms allow multiple users, so sharing an account can be a convenient and affordable solution.

Another area where you can save is on home maintenance services. Instead of hiring someone to clean your house or make small repairs, consider doing it yourself. There are many online resources, such as YouTube tutorials, that can teach you how to perform basic maintenance tasks. Not only will you save money, but you'll also gain valuable skills.

Finally, it's important to remember that you don't have to eliminate all conveniences from your life. The key is to find a balance. Decide which areas you are willing to pay for convenience and where you can go the extra mile to save money. Maybe you enjoy a delivered meal once a week, but decide to cook the rest of the time. Or maybe you opt to use public transportation during the week and only use transportation apps on the weekend.

In short, the cost of convenience may seem small at the time, but it adds up quickly and can seriously strain your budget. By being aware of these expenses and taking steps to reduce them, you can save a considerable amount of money without sacrificing too much of your comfort. Remember, every little savings counts, and at the end of the month, those small changes can make a big difference in your finances. It's time to take control of the cost of convenience and keep more money in your pocket!

Lucie Dupont

Lack of Planning in Purchases

We've all had that experience: going to the supermarket to buy a few things and leaving with a bag full of products that weren't on our list. The lack of planning in purchases is one of the main reasons why our expenses skyrocket without us realizing it. Shopping without a plan can lead to spending more than necessary, hoarding products we don't need, and ultimately taking a toll on our personal finances. In this chapter, we will explore how a lack of planning in purchases affects your budget and what strategies you can use to avoid these unnecessary expenses.

Lack of planning begins when we don't make a shopping list. Without a list, it's easy to wander the aisles of the supermarket, tempted by deals and products that aren't initially on our minds. Supermarkets are designed to attract our attention with eye-catching displays, promotions and strategically placed products to encourage impulse purchases. Without a clear list, we fall into the trap of adding things to the cart that we don't need.

Making a shopping list is a simple but effective step to control expenses. Before you go to the supermarket, take a few minutes to review what you really need. Check your pantry, refrigerator and cabinets to make sure you don't buy duplicates or things you already have at home. Write down everything you need on a list and commit to sticking to it. Not only will this help you save money, but it will also reduce the time you spend in the store, making your shopping experience more efficient.

Meal planning is also a powerful tool to avoid lack of planning when shopping. Set aside time each week to plan your meals and create a menu. By knowing exactly what ingredients you need for your meals, you can make a more accurate shopping list and avoid the temptation of buying things that aren't on your menu. This will not only help you spend less at the supermarket, but will also allow you to eat healthier and more varied.

Another effective strategy is to buy in large quantities only when necessary and beneficial. Although buying in bulk may seem like a good way to save money, it can lead to spending more if you're not careful. Only buy in bulk products that you use regularly and that do not spoil quickly. Also, make sure you have enough storage space at home for these products. Buying in bulk can be a great way to save, but only if you actually use what you buy.

Impulse purchases don't just happen at the supermarket. Clothing stores, shopping malls and online stores are full of temptations. Without proper planning, it's easy to spend more than planned on fashion items, gadgets, and other non-essential products. Before you go shopping, set a clear budget and commit to not spending more than you have allocated. If you see something you like but it wasn't on your list or budget, give yourself some time to think about the purchase. Many times, after a day or two, you will realize that you don't need that item.

Promotions and sales are another common trap when we do not plan our purchases. Buy one, get one free deals or limited-time discounts can be tempting, but only if you really need those products. Before taking advantage of a promotion, ask yourself if you really need the item and if you will use it. If the answer is no, then it is not a bargain, but an unnecessary expense.

Online shopping can be especially dangerous for those who don't plan. With just one click, you can buy anything from the comfort of your home. Online stores use tactics such as product suggestions, flash sales, and free shipping offers to encourage impulse purchases. To avoid these expenses, set a spending limit for your online purchases and use a wish list for items you're interested in. If after a few days you still want and need the item, then consider purchasing it. If not, you will have avoided an unnecessary purchase.

Lack of planning can also lead to additional expenses in the form of food waste. When we shop without a list or a plan, it's easy to end up with more food than we can consume before it goes bad. This is not only a waste of money, but also a waste of resources. Planning your meals and buying only what you need can significantly reduce food waste and save money.

In short, the lack of planning in purchases is one of the main reasons why we spend more than necessary. By making a shopping list, planning your meals, setting a budget, and avoiding impulse purchases, you can take control of your spending and keep more money in your pocket. Remember, every little savings counts, and at the end of the month, those small changes can make a big difference in your finances. It's time to plan your purchases and keep more money in your pocket!

Lucie Dupont

Inefficient Use of Resources

Often, without realizing it, we use resources inefficiently, which results in unnecessary spending of money. Whether we are wasting energy, water, food, or any other resource, this inefficiency can seriously affect our budget. In this chapter, we will explore how to identify and correct inefficient resource use in our daily lives to save money and be more sustainable.

One of the most common resources we use inefficiently is energy. From leaving lights on in empty rooms to keeping appliances plugged in when not in use, these small habits can add up to a high electric bill. Changing these habits can be simple but effective. Turning off lights when you leave a room, unplugging appliances when not in use, and using energy-saving light bulbs are easy ways to reduce your energy consumption. Plus, investing in energy-efficient appliances can mean significant savings in the long run, even if the initial cost is a little higher.

Inefficient water use is another area where we may be spending more than necessary. Leaking faucets and pipes, taking long showers, and overusing water for household chores are common examples.

Fixing leaks immediately, taking shorter showers, and using water-saving devices like shower heads and low-flow faucets can help reduce water consumption. Also, collecting rainwater to water plants and using a broom instead of a hose to clean sidewalks are simple ways to save water.

Heating and cooling your home can also be a source of inefficient resource use. Ensuring your home is well insulated can significantly reduce the amount of energy needed to maintain a comfortable temperature. Sealing windows and doors to prevent drafts, using thick curtains to keep warm in winter, and keeping windows closed during the day in summer are effective measures. Additionally, programming your thermostat to adjust the temperature when you're not home can reduce energy consumption without sacrificing your comfort.

Inefficiency in food use is another area that affects both our budget and the environment. Buying more food than we can consume before it spoils, not storing food properly, and not using leftovers are examples of this. Planning your meals and buying only what you need can significantly reduce food waste. Plus, learning how to store food correctly and finding creative ways to use leftovers can save you money and reduce waste.

Another resource that we often use inefficiently is time. Although time is not something we can directly measure in terms of money, its inefficient use can lead to unnecessary expenses. For example, not planning your tasks and appointments can result in multiple unnecessary trips, wasting more gas and time. Organizing your week, grouping tasks and planning efficient routes can help you save time and money.

Inefficient use of resources is not limited to households; It is also seen in purchases. Buying disposable items instead of reusable ones, opting for low-quality products that wear out quickly, and not taking advantage of sales and discounts are all ways we can spend more than necessary. Investing in good quality products, although initially more expensive, can result in long-term savings as you will not have to replace them as frequently. Plus, searching for deals, using coupons, and buying in bulk when appropriate can help you spend less.

Transportation is another area where we can be inefficient. Aggressive driving, failure to properly maintain your vehicle, and failure to plan trips can result in increased fuel consumption and higher repair costs. Driving smoothly and consistently, performing regular vehicle maintenance, and planning efficient routes can help reduce these costs.

In the technology space, we leave many electronic devices on standby or on when not in use, which consumes energy unnecessarily. Unplugging devices that are not in use, using smart power strips, and opting for devices with energy efficiency labels can significantly reduce energy consumption in your home.

Finally, clothing and other personal items can also be used inefficiently. Buying clothes we don't need or wear often, not properly caring for our clothes, and not repairing damaged items are ways to waste money. Buying less but better quality, learning to care for and repair your belongings, and donating or recycling what you no longer use can help you use your resources more efficiently.

In short, inefficient use of resources can have a significant impact on your finances. By being aware of how you use energy, water, food, time, and other resources, and taking steps to use them more efficiently, you can save a considerable amount of money. Remember, every little savings counts, and at the end of the month, those small changes can make a big difference in your finances. It's time to use your resources efficiently and keep more money in your pocket!

Don't Compare Prices

One of the most common mistakes we make when spending money is not comparing prices before making a purchase. This simple step may seem like a hassle, but the truth is that it can save you a considerable amount of money over time. Not comparing prices can result in paying more than necessary for the same products or services, and in this chapter we will explore how this habit affects your finances and what you can do to become a smarter shopper and save money.

Imagine you are in the supermarket and you see your favorite brand of cereal. Without thinking twice, you put it in your cart. However, if you had taken a few minutes to compare prices of other brands or even the same brand in different sizes, you could have found a cheaper option. Many times, stores place products from well-known brands at eye level, because they know that you are more likely to buy them without looking at other options. But by bending over or looking up, you could find similar products at a much lower price.

Price comparison doesn't just apply to supermarkets. Think about the times you have bought clothes, electronics, furniture or any other item without checking the prices in different stores. The price difference can be surprising. A t-shirt that costs $50 at one store may be available for $30 at another, or even cheaper if there is a sale or discount. With today's technology, comparing prices is easier than ever. There are apps and websites dedicated to price comparison that allow you to quickly see where you can find the best deal.

Not comparing prices also extends to services such as insurance, mobile telephony, internet and other subscription services. Many people stay with the same service provider for years without investigating whether there are cheaper options or better benefits available. Service providers often rely on the loyalty of their customers, but they also know that competition is fierce and may offer better prices or promotions to attract new customers. Taking time each year to review and compare these services can result in significant savings.

Another area where price comparison is crucial is in online shopping. Online shopping is convenient, but it can also lead to spending more if you don't take the time to compare prices. Different websites may offer the same product at different prices, and online price fluctuations can be frequent. Using browser extensions and price comparison sites can help you find the best deals and ensure you don't pay more than you have to.

Not comparing prices is also seen in everyday decisions. For example, when you decide to fill up your gas tank at the nearest station without checking prices at other nearby stations, you could be missing out on the opportunity to save a few dollars every time you fill up. The same goes for everyday items, such as cleaning products or toiletries. By shopping at the most convenient store without looking at other options, you could be paying more.

To avoid this expensive habit, here are some effective strategies for comparing prices and ensuring you get the best deal possible:

1. Make a shopping list: Before you go shopping, make a list of the items you need. This will help you maintain focus and avoid impulsive purchases.

2. Research online: Use price comparison websites and apps to see where you can find the products you need at a better price. Some apps even notify you when prices drop.

3. Take advantage of deals and coupons: Look for coupons and special offers before making a purchase. Many stores have regular discounts or promotions that can help you save money.

4. Buy in bulk: For products you use regularly, consider buying in bulk. Although the initial cost may be higher, the price per unit is usually lower.

5. Be flexible: If you are willing to be flexible with brands or stores, you can find better prices. Sometimes lesser-known brands offer products of equal or better quality at a lower price.

6. Check reviews: Reading reviews from other customers can help you determine if a product or service is worth the price. Reviews can give you an idea of the quality and durability of a product.

7. Sign up for alerts: Many online stores offer price alerts that will notify you when the price of a product drops. This can be useful for more expensive products or planned purchases.

8. Don't be afraid to negotiate: In some physical stores, you can try to negotiate the price, especially if you buy multiple items or if you have seen the same product for a lower price elsewhere.

9. Use discount cards: Many stores offer discount cards or loyalty programs that can provide you with additional savings on your purchases.

In short, not comparing prices is one of the easiest ways to lose money without realizing it. By taking the time to research and compare before purchasing, you can ensure you get the best value for your money. Every little savings counts, and at the end of the month, those small changes can make a big difference in your finances. It's time to become a smart shopper and keep more money in your pocket!

Lucie Dupont

Inadequate Insurance

Insurance is an essential tool to protect our finances against unforeseen events. However, having inadequate insurance can be almost as harmful as having none. Overpaying for unnecessary coverage or not having enough coverage in critical situations can result in wasted money and serious financial hardship. In this chapter, we'll explore how inadequate insurance can affect your budget and what you can do to ensure you have adequate protection without spending more than necessary.

When we talk about inadequate insurance, we're talking about two main situations: overpaying for coverage you don't need and not having enough coverage for the risks you face. Both situations can have a significant impact on your finances. First, let's look at the problem of overpaying for insurance.

You may have purchased an insurance policy years ago and your needs have changed since then. Maybe you have an auto insurance policy with collision coverage that was necessary when you had a new car, but now your vehicle is many years old and its value has decreased significantly. In this case, continuing to pay for comprehensive coverage may not be the best financial decision. Reviewing your policies regularly and adjusting coverages based on your current needs can help you save money.

Additionally, some people purchase additional coverages without really understanding if they need them. For example, your health insurance may offer coverage for treatments or services that you will never use, such as maternity insurance for someone who does not plan to have children. Review your policies and make sure you are paying only for the coverage you really need. Talking to an insurance agent can help you better understand your options and adjust your policy to your specific needs.

The other side of the problem is not having enough coverage. Imagine that you have home insurance that does not adequately cover the value of your property or the belongings within it. In the event of a disaster, such as a fire or flood, you could find yourself in a situation where the repair or replacement costs far exceed the amount your policy covers, leaving you with large out-of-pocket expenses. Having insufficient coverage can result in huge financial problems when you need help most.

It's crucial to evaluate your needs and make sure you have enough coverage. For example, if you have dependents, adequate life insurance can ensure that they are financially protected should something happen to you. Without adequate coverage, your loved ones could face financial hardship. Likewise, health insurance that doesn't cover certain important treatments or procedures can leave you with large medical bills in the event of an illness or accident.

An important aspect to consider is the deductible of your policy. The deductible is the amount you must pay out of pocket before insurance begins to cover the costs. Choosing a higher deductible can lower your monthly premiums, but make sure you can afford to pay that amount in an emergency. Balancing the cost of premiums and the deductible is essential to finding a policy that fits your budget and needs.

Additionally, it is important to compare different insurance options and providers. Not all insurance companies offer the same coverage or prices, so taking the time to research and compare can help you find the best option. Using online tools, talking to multiple agents, and reading reviews from other customers can give you a better idea of which policy is best for you.

Don't forget to review your insurance policies regularly. Insurance needs can change over time due to changes in your life, such as buying a new home, having children, changing jobs, or even improving your health. Reviewing and adjusting your policies annually can ensure that you always have adequate coverage without overpaying.

In addition to traditional insurance such as life, health, home and auto, consider other types of insurance that may be relevant to your situation. For example, if you travel frequently, travel insurance can protect you against cancellations, lost luggage, or medical emergencies abroad. If you own a business, business insurance can protect you against losses and liabilities.

In short, having inadequate insurance can be a waste of money and leave you vulnerable at critical times. To ensure you have the right coverage, review your needs regularly, adjust your policies as necessary, compare options and providers, and consult with an insurance agent for guidance. By doing so, you can protect your finances and ensure that you are prepared for any eventuality without overspending. It's time to take control of your insurance and make sure every penny you spend on it is well spent!

Not Planning for the Future

One of the most common and costly financial mistakes we can make is not planning for the future. Many people live day to day, worrying only about immediate expenses and leaving aside the importance of thinking about tomorrow. Without proper planning, it is easy to find yourself in difficult financial situations, especially when emergencies arise or retirement arrives. In this chapter, we'll explore how a lack of planning can affect your finances and how you can take steps to ensure you're prepared for the future.

Living without financial planning is like sailing a ship without direction. Without a clear plan, it's easy to get sidetracked and lose sight of your goals. One of the most important aspects of financial planning is setting clear and achievable goals. These goals may include saving for retirement, buying a home, paying for your children's education, or simply building an emergency fund. Without concrete goals, it's difficult to measure your progress and stay motivated to save and spend responsibly.

A crucial aspect of financial planning is creating a budget. A budget helps you control your income and expenses, making sure you don't spend more than you earn. Many people underestimate the importance of a budget, but it is an essential tool for managing your finances. By creating a budget, you can identify areas where you can cut unnecessary spending and direct those funds toward your long-term financial goals.

In addition to the budget, it is important to have an emergency fund. Life is full of unexpected events, and an emergency fund can protect you from unexpected situations like a job loss, illness, or an expensive home repair. Without an emergency fund, you could be forced to resort to credit cards or loans, racking up debt that can be difficult to pay off. It is recommended to have at least three to six months of essential expenses saved in an emergency fund.

Another key area of financial planning is retirement. As we age, it is essential to think about how we will support ourselves once we stop working. Relying solely on government pensions or last-minute savings is not enough. Starting to save for retirement as early as possible can make a big difference. Contributing regularly to a pension plan or individual retirement account (IRA) can help you accumulate enough funds to maintain your lifestyle in retirement. Taking advantage of employer contributions, if available, is also a great way to boost your savings.

In addition to saving for retirement, it is essential to consider estate planning and insurance. Having a will and designating beneficiaries for your financial accounts can ensure that your wishes are carried out and your loved ones are protected. Also, making sure you have adequate life insurance can provide financial security for your family in case something happens to you.

Education is another important aspect of planning for the future. If you have children, you probably want to support their education. Starting to save for college as soon as possible can help you avoid the financial burden of student loans. There are education savings plans, such as 529 plans, that offer tax advantages and can help you accumulate funds for your children's education.

Planning for the future also includes debt management. Having debt can be a significant burden that affects your ability to save and spend responsibly. Creating a plan to pay off your debt as quickly as possible can free you from this burden and allow you to focus on other financial goals. Prioritizing paying off high-interest debt and avoiding accumulating new debt are essential steps to successful financial planning.

Investing is another important part of planning for the future. Although saving is crucial, investing your money can help you grow your wealth over time. There are many investment options, from stocks and bonds to real estate and mutual funds. Diversifying your investments and consulting with a financial advisor can help you make informed decisions and minimize risks.

Finally, financial education is essential for long-term planning. Learning about personal finance, investing, taxes, and estate planning can give you the tools you need to make informed decisions. There are many resources available, from books and online courses to professional financial advice. Taking time to improve your financial literacy can have a significant impact on your ability to plan and achieve your financial goals.

In short, failing to plan for the future can result in serious financial hardship and limit your opportunities. Taking steps to set clear goals, create a budget, save for emergencies and retirement, manage debt, invest, and improve your financial literacy can help you ensure a stable and prosperous financial future. It's time to take control of your finances and plan for a better future!

Lucie Dupont

Lack of Financial Education

Lack of financial education is one of the biggest obstacles we face when it comes to managing our money effectively. Without adequate knowledge, it is easy to make mistakes that can cost us dearly, from accumulating unnecessary debt to missing savings and investment opportunities. In this chapter, we will explore how a lack of financial education impacts our lives and what we can do to improve our understanding of money management.

Financial education refers to the knowledge and skills necessary to make informed decisions about our money. This includes understanding how budgeting, saving, investing, taxes, and insurance work. Unfortunately, many people do not receive this education in school or at home, leaving them ill-prepared to face the financial challenges of adult life.

One of the most common problems resulting from a lack of financial education is the inability to make an effective budget. A budget is an essential tool that helps us control our income and expenses, ensuring that we don't spend more than we earn. Without a budget, it's easy to lose control of our finances, rack up debt, and live paycheck to paycheck. Learning how to create and follow a budget is a crucial first step for anyone looking to improve their financial situation.

Lack of financial education can also lead us to accumulate debt irresponsibly. Many people don't fully understand how credit cards and loans work, and end up using these tools without thinking about the long-term consequences. The result can be a debt load that becomes difficult to manage, with high interest that consumes much of our income. Understanding how interest rates work and how to calculate debt payments can help us make more informed decisions and avoid financial problems.

Another critical aspect of financial education is savings. Without a proper understanding of the importance of saving, many people live in the present without thinking about the future. Whether for an emergency fund, buying a home or retirement, saving is essential to ensure our long-term financial stability. Learning how to save effectively, setting savings goals, and understanding different savings account options can help us build a solid financial foundation.

Investing is another topic that is often overlooked due to lack of financial education. Many people are afraid to invest because they don't understand how the stock market, bonds, mutual funds, and other investment options work. However, investing is one of the best ways to grow our money in the long term. Learning the basics of investing and how to diversify our investments can help us make safer decisions and increase our wealth.

In addition to these aspects, financial education also includes understanding how taxes work. Paying taxes is an inevitable part of life, but many people don't fully understand how they are calculated and what tax deductions or credits they can take advantage of. This lack of knowledge can lead to paying more than necessary in taxes or facing problems with the IRS. Learning about the tax system and how to properly file our tax returns can save us money and trouble in the future.

Insurance is another area where a lack of financial education can be costly. Whether it's health, life, car or home insurance, understanding what type of coverage we need and how policies work is essential to protecting ourselves against unexpected risks. Without this knowledge, we can end up overpaying for unnecessary coverage or, worse yet, facing situations where we don't have adequate protection when we need it most.

Retirement planning is another crucial aspect that is often neglected due to lack of financial education. Many people don't start saving for retirement until it is too late, which can result in retirement without enough money to maintain their desired lifestyle. Understanding how pension plans, IRAs, and other retirement savings vehicles work can help us better prepare for the future.

Fortunately, it is never too late to improve our financial education. There are many resources available to learn about personal finance, from books and online courses to workshops and professional financial advice. Taking time to improve our financial knowledge can have a significant impact on our ability to manage money effectively and achieve our financial goals.

Here are some strategies to improve your financial education:

1. Read personal finance books: There are many excellent books that cover a wide range of financial topics, from budgeting to investing and retirement planning.

2. Take online courses: There are many free and paid online courses that offer financial education, from educational platforms to financial institution websites.

3. Use financial management applications: Financial management applications can help you control your expenses, create budgets and save money. Some even offer personalized financial advice.

4. Consult a financial advisor: If you have specific questions or need help planning your finances, a financial advisor can offer expert, personalized guidance.

5. Participate in workshops and seminars: Many communities and organizations offer

workshops and seminars on personal finance. These events can provide you with valuable information and the opportunity to ask questions to experts.

6. Follow financial blogs and podcasts: There are many blogs and podcasts dedicated to financial education that offer practical advice and updates on financial topics.

7. Practice what you learn: The best way to improve your financial education is to apply what you learn in your daily life. Create a budget, open a savings account, invest in the stock market, and continually educate yourself.

In short, a lack of financial education can have serious consequences for our personal finances. Without proper knowledge, it is easy to make mistakes that cost us money and limit our opportunities to achieve our financial goals. By taking steps to improve our financial education, we can take control of our finances, avoid problems, and ensure a more stable and prosperous financial future. It's time to invest in your financial education and build a solid foundation for your financial well-being!

Lucie Dupont

Entertainment Expenses

Entertainment is an essential part of our lives. It helps us relax, enjoy and connect with others. However, entertainment expenses can quickly become a large financial burden if not managed properly. In this chapter, we'll explore how the costs associated with entertainment can affect your finances, and what steps you can take to enjoy life without overspending.

Entertainment covers a wide range of activities, from dining out, going to the movies, concerts, subscriptions to streaming services, to vacations and travel. All of these expenses, although necessary for our emotional and social well-being, can add up quickly and affect our budget if we do not control them. For example, a weekly trip to the movies with friends may seem harmless, but if you add up the cost of tickets, popcorn, and soft drinks, you could be spending a considerable amount of money each month.

A common mistake is not planning for entertainment expenses and simply paying for these activities when they arise. Without a clear entertainment budget, it's easy to spend more than we can really afford. The key is to set a specific monthly entertainment budget and stick to it. This doesn't mean you should give up all fun activities, but rather find a balance that allows you to enjoy yourself without compromising your finances.

Subscriptions to streaming services and other online services are another example of how entertainment expenses can add up without us realizing it. It is common to subscribe to multiple services such as Netflix, Hulu, Disney+, Amazon Prime, among others, thinking that each one offers something unique. However, when you add up all of these subscriptions, you could be spending a significant amount of money each month. One solution is to regularly review your subscriptions and cancel those you don't use frequently. You can also consider sharing accounts with family or friends to split the costs.

Eating out is another area where entertainment spending can get out of control. Eating in restaurants is a pleasant experience, but it can be very expensive if done too frequently. Instead of eating out several times a week, consider eating out only on special occasions. Additionally, you can look for cheaper alternatives, such as preparing meals at home and organizing dinners with friends or family. Cooking together is not only cheaper, but it can also be a fun and social activity.

Live events, such as concerts and shows, can also represent a considerable expense. It's tempting to buy tickets to see your favorite band or attend a sporting event, but these expenses can add up quickly. To control these costs, set a limit on how much you're willing to spend on live events each year and carefully choose which ones to attend. Look for discounts or promotions and buy tickets in advance for better prices.

Vacations and travel are another big source of entertainment spending. Traveling is an enriching experience, but it can be very expensive if not planned properly. To save money on travel, consider traveling during the off-season, look for deals and discounts, and opt for cheaper accommodations, such as vacation rentals or guesthouses. You can also plan vacations closer to home to reduce transportation costs.

Another strategy to reduce entertainment expenses is to take advantage of the free or low-cost activities your community offers. Many cities have free events, such as outdoor concerts, festivals, art exhibitions, and park recreation. Stay informed about these events and make an effort to participate in them. Not only will you save money, but you will also be able to enjoy new and exciting experiences.

In addition to these strategies, it is important to be aware of how and why you spend on entertainment. Ask yourself if you really enjoy every activity you spend money on or if you do it out of habit or social pressure. Sometimes simply being more mindful of your spending decisions can help you cut costs without feeling like you're depriving yourself of something.

A useful tool for managing entertainment expenses is the use of budgeting apps. These apps can help you track your spending in real time, set limits, and receive alerts when you get close to your budget. Some apps even offer recommendations on how to save money on different spending categories.

Another idea is to plan entertainment activities that don't involve spending money. For example, you can host game nights at home, have movie marathons with friends, explore nature trails, or do creative activities like painting or writing. These activities can be just as fun and rewarding without the cost associated with traditional outings.

In short, entertainment expenses can quickly add up and strain your budget if not managed properly. The key is to be aware of your expenses, establish a specific budget for entertainment and look for cheaper alternatives without sacrificing fun. By doing so, you can enjoy a full and exciting life without compromising your finances. It's time to take control of your entertainment spending and find creative ways to enjoy life without overspending!

Lucie Dupont

Gifts and Celebrations

Gifts and celebrations are an important part of our lives. They allow us to express our love and appreciation for others, celebrate special moments and create unforgettable memories. However, these events can also be a significant source of expenses if we do not manage them properly. In this chapter, we'll explore how the costs associated with gift-giving and celebrations can affect your finances and how you can enjoy these special moments without overspending.

Gifts are a beautiful way to show our love and appreciation, but it's easy to get carried away and spend more than we can afford. Important dates like birthdays, anniversaries, weddings, and holidays can add up quickly in terms of gift spending. One way to control these costs is to plan ahead. Making a list of the people you want to give gifts to and setting a budget for each gift can help you stay within your financial limits. Plus, keeping an eye out for sales and discounts throughout the year can help you find gifts at better prices.

Celebrations, such as birthday parties, anniversaries, and family reunions, can also be expensive. Venue rental, food, drinks, decor and entertainment can add up quickly. To keep these expenses under control, consider cheaper alternatives. For example, instead of renting a venue, host the celebration at home or in a park. Ask your guests to bring a plate to share, which will not only reduce costs but also add variety to the meal. Also, instead of hiring professional entertainment, look for fun activities that you can organize yourself, such as board games, karaoke, or a movie night.

Holidays, such as Christmas, New Year's, Valentine's Day, and other holidays, can also mean a lot of spending on gifts, decorations, and special foods. One way to reduce these costs is to set a specific budget for each holiday and stick to it. Consider doing gift exchanges instead of buying gifts for each person. Not only does this reduce expenses, but it can also be a fun and exciting activity for everyone involved. Plus, making your own decorations and foods can be an inexpensive and creative way to celebrate.

Handmade gifts are a great way to show your love without spending a lot of money. Making something with your own hands is not only more personal, but it can also be more meaningful to the person receiving the gift. From baking cookies to knitting a scarf or making a personalized card, there are plenty of ways to get creative and save money at the same time.

Another strategy to control spending on gifts and celebrations is to set clear expectations with your friends and family. Talk openly about the importance of staying on a budget and suggest cheaper alternatives for celebrating together. Often, you'll find that others are also looking for ways to reduce expenses and will be happy to work with you.

Greeting cards and gift wrapping can also add up in terms of expenses. Instead of purchasing expensive cards, consider making them yourself or sending them electronically. For gift wrapping, reuse wrapping paper, gift bags or boxes from previous celebrations, or use recyclable materials such as newspapers or fabrics.

Planning ahead is key to managing spending on gifts and celebrations. Creating an annual calendar of important events and allocating a budget for each will help you avoid last-minute expenses and take advantage of sales and discounts. Plus, saving a little each month for these events can ease financial pressure when it comes time to celebrate.

In short, gifts and celebrations are an important part of our lives, but they can represent a financial burden if not managed properly. Planning ahead, setting a budget, looking for cheaper alternatives, and being creative are effective strategies to enjoy these special moments without overspending. By taking control of your spending on gifts and celebrations, you can ensure that these events are memorable and meaningful without compromising your financial stability. Celebrate with joy and responsibility, and enjoy every moment without worrying about the cost!

The Cost of Health and Wellness

Health and well-being are essential to leading a full and satisfying life. Investing in our health allows us to enjoy a better quality of life and prevent long-term diseases. However, the costs associated with health and wellness care can be high and often difficult to manage. In this chapter, we will explore how these costs can affect our finances and what strategies we can adopt to take care of our health without overspending.

One of the main health-related expenses is health insurance. Having adequate insurance is crucial to protecting us against unexpected medical expenses, but monthly premiums, co-pays and deductibles can be a significant financial burden. To reduce these costs, it is important to compare different insurance plans and choose one that fits your needs and budget. If you have a job that offers health benefits, be sure to take full advantage of available options, such as health savings accounts (HSAs) or flexible spending accounts (FSAs), which can help you save money on medical expenses.

Doctor visits and medical treatments can also be expensive, especially if you do not have adequate health insurance. To control these expenses, it is important to schedule regular check-ups and maintain a good relationship with your primary care doctor. Preventing illness through regular checkups and maintaining a healthy lifestyle can reduce the need for expensive treatments in the long term. Additionally, look for clinics and health services that offer reduced or tiered rates based on your income.

Medications are another area where costs can add up quickly. Whether prescription or over-the-counter medications, it is essential to look for ways to reduce these expenses. Compare prices at different pharmacies and consider using generic medications, which are often much cheaper than name brands. If you take medications regularly, research patient assistance programs that may offer discounts or financial assistance.

Mental health is a crucial part of overall well-being, but the cost of mental health therapy and services can be prohibitive for many people. Fortunately, there are more affordable options available. Look for therapists who offer income-sensitive rates or free services at community organizations. Additionally, some apps and online programs offer mental health resources and support at little or no cost.

Physical wellness also involves staying fit through regular exercise, but the costs of gyms, fitness classes, and exercise equipment can add up. To reduce these expenses, consider cheaper or free options, such as exercising at home with online videos, joining community exercise groups, or taking advantage of public facilities such as parks and running tracks. Additionally, you can look for deals and discounts on gym memberships or fitness classes.

Healthy eating is essential for well-being, but it can be costly if not planned properly. Buying fresh, nutritious foods instead of processed foods may seem expensive, but there are ways to save on grocery shopping. Plan your meals in advance, make a shopping list, and take advantage of deals and discounts at the supermarket. Buying products in season and in bulk can also help you reduce costs. Also, consider growing your own vegetables and herbs at home if you have the space and time.

Dental health is another area where costs can be high, especially if you need treatments such as fillings, crowns or implants. To keep costs down, it is important to maintain good dental hygiene and visit the dentist regularly for preventive cleanings and checkups. Research dental insurance plans that can help cover some of the costs and look for dental clinics that offer reduced fees or financial assistance programs.

Preventative care is one of the best ways to control health and wellness costs. Adopting healthy habits, such as exercising regularly, eating a balanced diet, not smoking, and limiting alcohol consumption, can help you avoid long-term health problems and reduce the need for expensive medical treatments. Also, be sure to get vaccinated and follow public health recommendations to prevent illness.

Another way to save on health costs is to be an informed consumer. Research and compare prices for medical treatments, medications and health services. Don't hesitate to ask your doctor about cheaper alternatives and make sure you fully understand the costs before agreeing to any treatment.

In addition to these strategies, consider investing in programs and resources that promote overall well-being, such as stress management classes, meditation programs, or healthy cooking classes. These resources can help you maintain a healthy lifestyle and prevent long-term health problems.

In short, the cost of health and wellness can be significant, but there are many ways to manage these expenses effectively. By comparing insurance, planning doctor visits, looking for cheaper alternatives, and adopting healthy habits, you can take care of your health without compromising your finances. Remember that investing in your health is an investment in your future, and with a little planning and creativity, you can stay healthy and financially stable. Take care of your health and well-being without spending more and enjoy a full and healthy life!

Maintenance and repairs

Maintenance and repairs are an inevitable part of life. Whether it's your home, car, or any other property, there will always be things that need to be fixed or maintained. Although these expenses may seem small and sporadic, they can add up quickly and affect your finances if not managed properly. In this chapter, we'll explore how maintenance and repair costs can affect your budget and what strategies you can adopt to manage them effectively.

One of the main maintenance expenses is that of your home. Homes require constant maintenance to make sure everything is working properly and prevent major problems in the long run. From the heating and air conditioning system, to the roof and plumbing, there are many things that may need attention. The key to managing these costs is to be proactive. Performing regular inspections and addressing small problems before they become big ones can save you a lot of money. For example, a roof leak may seem minor, but if not fixed in time, it can cause significant damage that will be much more expensive to repair.

For car owners, vehicle maintenance and repairs are inevitable. Oil changes, tire rotations, and brake replacement are just a few of the regular services your car needs to stay in good shape. Ignoring this maintenance can result in more serious and costly breakdowns. It is advisable to follow the maintenance schedule suggested by the manufacturer and perform periodic inspections to avoid major problems. Plus, learning to do some maintenance tasks yourself, like changing the oil or filters, can help you save money.

The appliances and electronic equipment in your home also require occasional maintenance and repairs. Refrigerators, washers, dryers and televisions all have a lifespan and will eventually need to be repaired or replaced. To prolong the life of your appliances, be sure to follow the manufacturer's instructions for use and maintenance. Regularly cleaning filters and doing basic checks can prevent premature failures. When something breaks, evaluate whether it is more cost-effective to repair or replace the equipment. In some cases, repairing an appliance may be cheaper in the short term, but replacing it with a more energy-efficient one can save you money in the long run.

In addition to routine maintenance, emergency repairs can also represent a significant expense. A water heater that breaks down in the middle of winter or a pipe that breaks and causes flooding are examples of problems that require immediate attention. To prepare for these unexpected expenses, it is helpful to have an emergency fund. This fund should be large enough to cover several months of essential expenses and can help you handle emergency repairs without having to resort to loans or credit cards.

An effective strategy for managing maintenance and repair costs is to plan and budget for these expenses. Allocate a portion of your monthly budget specifically for maintenance and repairs. This will allow you to have money available when problems arise and will prevent these expenses from unbalancing your finances. Additionally, keeping a record of repairs and maintenance performed can help you anticipate when future interventions will be needed and plan accordingly.

It is also important to be an informed consumer. Do your research and compare prices before hiring a professional to perform repairs. Get several quotes and check references before making a decision. In some cases, you can find discounts or promotions that help you reduce costs. Additionally, consider contracting regular maintenance service for certain equipment, such as your heating and air conditioning system. These services are usually cheaper in the long run and can prevent major problems.

Prevention is one of the best ways to reduce maintenance and repair costs. Adopting habits that extend the life of your belongings can save you a lot of money. For example, keeping your car clean and protected from the elements can prevent wear and corrosion. In your home, avoiding excessive use of appliances and following the recommendations for proper use can prevent premature breakdowns. It's also helpful to watch for signs of problems and address them immediately. A strange noise in your car's engine or a damp spot on the wall of your house are signs that something needs attention.

Finally, consider learning some basic DIY skills. You don't need to be an expert, but learning how to make simple repairs can save you a lot of money in labor costs. There are many online resources, such as video tutorials and step-by-step guides, that can teach you how to perform basic maintenance and repair tasks. Even something as simple as knowing how to change a fuse or fix a small water leak can make a big difference in your finances.

In short, maintenance and repairs are unavoidable expenses, but with proper planning and some effective strategies, you can manage them without negatively affecting your finances. Being proactive, budgeting, research, and learning basic DIY skills are ways to keep these costs under control. By doing so, you can ensure that your home, car, and other belongings stay in good condition without overspending. Take care of your properties and finances, and enjoy the peace of mind of knowing that you are prepared for any eventuality!

Taxes and Declarations

Taxes are an inevitable reality in our lives. Whether you are self-employed or employed, you will always have to pay taxes. Understanding how taxes work and how to handle tax returns is essential to ensure you are not paying more than necessary. In this chapter, we're going to explore how taxes and filings can affect your finances and how you can handle these processes effectively to save money.

Taxes may seem complicated, but understanding the basics can help you handle them better. There are different types of taxes that affect your finances, such as income tax, sales tax, and property taxes. Income tax is one of the most significant and is based on your annual income. The more you earn, the more taxes you pay, but there are also tax deductions and credits that can reduce the amount you owe.

Tax deductions are expenses that you can subtract from your taxable income, reducing the amount of income you pay taxes on. For example, if you work from home, you can deduct some of your home office expenses. Other common examples of deductions include student loan interest, medical expenses, and contributions to retirement plans. Making the most of tax deductions can mean considerable savings.

Tax credits, on the other hand, are even more beneficial than deductions because they directly reduce the amount of taxes you must pay. For example, the child credit allows you to reduce your taxes if you have children under a certain age. Other tax credits may be available for education, retirement savings, and adoption, among others. Be sure to research and claim all tax credits you are entitled to to maximize your savings.

The key to managing your taxes effectively is planning. Don't wait until the last minute to organize your documents and file your return. Keep a detailed record of all your income and expenses throughout the year. Not only will this make it easier for you when it comes time to file, but it will also help you identify opportunities for tax deductions and credits.

Hiring a tax professional can be a valuable investment, especially if your finances are complex. An experienced accountant or tax preparer can help you find deductions and credits you might have overlooked and make sure your tax return is accurate. Although there is a cost associated with hiring a professional, the potential tax savings and stress relief may be worth it.

For those who prefer to handle their taxes on their own, there are many tax preparation tools and software available. These programs can guide you through the process step by step, help you find deductions and credits, and ensure your return is accurate. Make sure you choose software that is reliable and up-to-date with the latest tax laws.

Another important aspect of taxes is compliance. Failure to file your taxes on time or pay the correct amount can result in fines and penalties. If you are having difficulty paying your taxes, contact the tax authority as soon as possible to discuss payment options. Ignoring the problem will only make things worse and increase your costs in the long run.

It's important to understand that taxes aren't something that just disappears after you file your return. Tax planning should be an ongoing part of your financial strategy. For example, adjusting your tax withholdings at your job can help you avoid surprises at the end of the year. If you're receiving a large refund, it could be a sign that you're withholding too much from your paychecks and you could adjust your withholdings to have more money available each month.

For self-employed people and small business owners, taxes can be even more complicated. In addition to income tax, you should also consider self-employment taxes, which cover Medicare and Social Security. Keeping accurate records of your income and expenses is crucial to avoiding problems with the IRS and ensuring you are paying the correct amount of taxes.

Investments also have tax implications. Dividends, capital gains, and interest earned on investments are taxable. Strategically planning your investments can help you minimize your taxes. For example, holding investments for the long term rather than selling quickly can reduce your capital gains taxes.

Finally, it is important to be aware of changes in tax laws. Tax laws change regularly and can have a significant impact on your finances. Stay informed about new laws and how they may affect you. Consider subscribing to tax newsletters or consulting with a tax professional regularly to make sure you're taking advantage of every opportunity to save on taxes.

In short, taxes and filings can be a significant financial burden, but with proper planning and an informed approach, you can manage them effectively. Taking advantage of tax deductions and credits, keeping accurate records, considering hiring a professional, and staying informed about tax laws are key strategies to minimize your costs and avoid problems with the IRS. By taking control of your taxes, you can ensure you're paying only what you owe and keep more money in your pocket. Plan, organize and maximize your tax savings for a healthier and more balanced financial life!

Lucie Dupont

Periodic Evaluation and Adjustments

Maintaining control of your finances is not a one-time task; It is a continuous process that requires periodic evaluation and adjustments. This chapter is dedicated to the importance of regularly reviewing your finances and making the necessary changes to ensure you are on the right path toward your financial goals. Let's explore how you can evaluate your financial situation and what adjustments you can make to improve your financial well-being.

Regularly evaluating your finances is essential to understand where you are and where you are going. This involves reviewing all your income, expenses, savings and investments. One of the first things you should do is create a detailed budget, if you haven't already. A budget allows you to clearly see how much money comes in and goes out each month. It is an essential tool for identifying areas where you may be overspending and where you can save.

A good practice is to review your budget at least once a month. This will help you make sure you're sticking to your financial plan and allow you to make quick adjustments if you notice any deviations. For example, if you realize that you are spending more than planned on entertainment, you can look for ways to reduce those expenses in the next month. The key is to be honest with yourself and be willing to make the changes necessary to keep your finances in order.

Another important aspect of financial evaluation is to review your short- and long-term goals. Ask yourself if you are making progress toward your goals and if those goals are still relevant. Financial goals can change over time, and it's important to adjust them based on your current circumstances. For example, if your goal was to save for a trip and you have already achieved it, you can set a new goal, such as saving for your children's education or for the purchase of a home.

Part of the evaluation also involves reviewing your debts. Keep track of how much you owe and who you owe. Evaluate the interest rates and conditions of each debt. If you have high-interest debt, consider consolidating it or finding ways to pay it off more quickly. Reducing your debt can free up money that you can use for other purposes, such as saving or investing.

Reviewing your investments is another crucial part of periodic evaluation. Make sure your investments are aligned with your financial goals and risk tolerance. Financial markets can be volatile, and what worked a few years ago may not be the best option now. Consult a financial advisor if necessary and make appropriate adjustments to keep your investment portfolio balanced and oriented toward your goals.

An often overlooked aspect of financial evaluation is reviewing your insurance. Make sure you have the right coverage for your current situation. This includes health, life, home, and auto insurance. Insurance needs can change over time, so it's important to review your policies and adjust them as necessary. For example, if you've paid off your mortgage, you may no longer need as much life insurance.

In addition to monthly evaluations, it is helpful to do a more thorough financial review at least once a year. During this annual review, you can take a deeper look at your spending habits, long-term goals, and any significant changes to your income or expenses. This is also a good time to review your tax return and plan for the next tax year. Take the opportunity to adjust your tax withholding if necessary and make sure you are taking advantage of all available tax deductions and credits.

Technology can be a great ally in the financial evaluation process. There are many apps and online tools that can help you track your expenses, create budgets, and monitor your investments. Using these tools can make the evaluation process easier and more efficient. Additionally, many of these apps can send you alerts and reminders, helping you stay on track with your regular checkups.

It is important to involve your family in the financial evaluation and adjustment process. If you have a partner or children, make sure everyone is aware of the financial situation and working together toward common goals. Open communication and collaboration can make it easier to stay on track and make adjustments when necessary.

Financial assessment and adjustments are not just for when things go wrong. Even if you're in a good financial position, it's crucial to keep reviewing and adjusting your plan. Circumstances change, and what works today may not be effective tomorrow. Staying proactive and flexible will allow you to adapt to any changes and continue moving towards your goals.

In short, periodic evaluation and adjustments are essential for effective management of your finances. Creating and reviewing a budget, analyzing your debt, monitoring your investments, reviewing your insurance, and planning your taxes are key steps in this process. Use technology to facilitate reviews and maintain open communication with your family about finances. By making financial assessment a regular practice, you can ensure that you are on the right path to a healthy and prosperous financial life. Remember, the key to financial success is consistency and adaptability!

Lucie Dupont